Mandla Khumalo

Overcoming opposition

Mandla Khumalo

Overcoming opposition

A spiritual guide to attaining peace in hard times

Blessed Hope Publishing

Imprint

Any brand names and product names mentioned in this book are subject to trademark, brand or patent protection and are trademarks or registered trademarks of their respective holders. The use of brand names, product names, common names, trade names, product descriptions etc. even without a particular marking in this work is in no way to be construed to mean that such names may be regarded as unrestricted in respect of trademark and brand protection legislation and could thus be used by anyone.

Cover image: www.ingimage.com

Publisher:
Blessed Hope Publishing
is a trademark of
Dodo Books Indian Ocean Ltd. and OmniScriptum S.R.L publishing group

120 High Road, East Finchley, London, N2 9ED, United Kingdom
Str. Armeneasca 28/1, office 1, Chisinau MD-2012, Republic of Moldova, Europe
Printed at: see last page
ISBN: 978-620-4-18818-8

OVERCOMING OPPOSITION

By

MANDLA KHUMALO

2024

The inscrutabilities untold shall be revealed

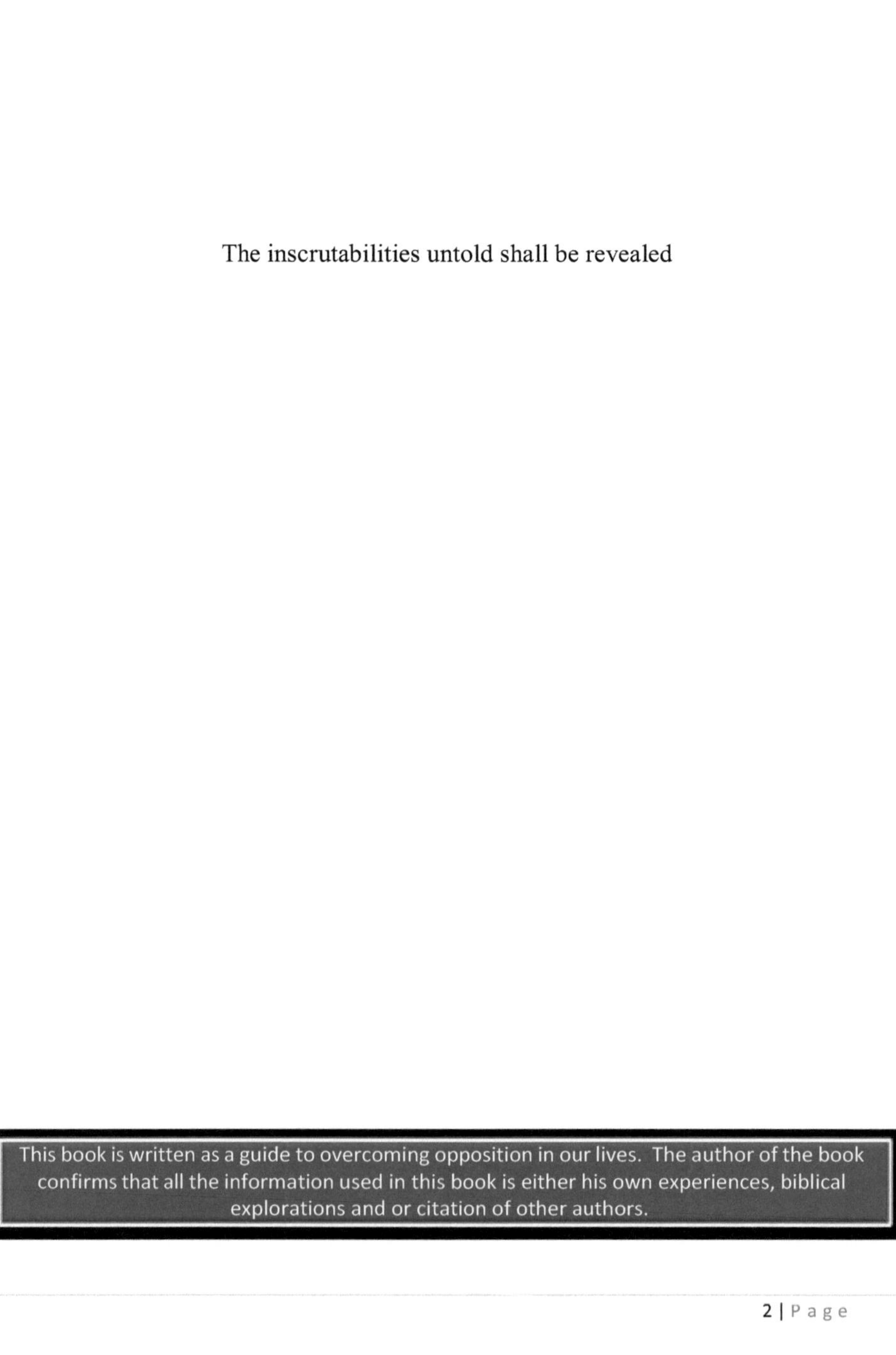

Table of Contents   **Page**

DEDICATION

This book is dedicated to Sindisiwe Gama my queen and my love, who has constantly been on my corner and always encouraging me to continue with my Studies.

ACKNOWLEDGEMENTS

To the Almighty God who sustains and embellishes His people, I have no words sufficient to give You the glory due to You. I'm only just a little pebble in your hands always ready to be thrown. Wherever you throw me magnificent Saviour I will go for I have comprehended that it's not about me but about the unseen mysteries prevalent in my life. You are the Captain of my ship. To Bishop Professor Patrick Phakathi, the journey is only beginning man of the most High God. Thank you for your guidance and the opportunity you have opened for God's people. The eyes behind eyes prevalent in you and your wife are unexplainable. Thank you again even for your prayer support. A tunnel leads to a different destination, potentially far better than the conversant environment. The journey seen in the spirit shall be revealed in the physical. I know you understand these words.

To my brother Vusi Khumalo and my mother thank you so much for your support. And to the children Majaha, Temantungwa, and Aphiwe we hope you get to publish better books and theses than we did. Much love bo Khumalo. Lastly to the storms and winds, remember that the light shines in darkness and the darkness does not comprehend it. To the Zwakele, Vuyolwethu, Molly and Sthobela, journey shall begin.

1.0 INTRODUCTION

Life is a mystery and no one can fully comprehend it. The birth, growth, maturing and death of a human being is something researchers are still trying to understand and apparently no one can fully grasp such a marvelous yet hidden pillar. The very beginning is something which is still debated even to the very day and age. The prospects of evolution are rampant amongst biologist and the concept of creation is strongly believed by theologians drawing their conclusions from the guiding book which is the bible. In biology, evolution is the change in the characteristics of a species over several generations and relies on the process of natural selection. It is a concept based on the idea that all species are related and gradually change over time (Darwin, 2017). The shortfall of the evolution concept is that although it makes sense to the ones who believe in it, but they cannot fully explain why is not happening today. They conclude that a human being was a result of evolution. To be precise their conclusions specify that human being were as a result of monkey miraculously changing into humans due to unknown forces. One wonders if such forces are no longer in place nowadays to cause the people to evolve into something else beyond being humans. If they were able to evolve from being monkeys into humans, surely they can still evolve into something else. Monkeys are still present even today. We hardly hear of them evolving into humans in the present age. This then brings a lot of debate in the research space. On the other hand the concept of creation seems to be making sense. The annals of the bible seem to present details of how things really unfolded. According to Richard (2022) the doctrine of creation states that God, who alone was uncreated and is eternal, formed and gave existence to everything outside of Himself. All this was done through the word of his power and all of it was very good.

Life is a greatest gift given to humanity and there is no argument there. There are a lot of thrills, opportunities, trials and tribulations associated with such a superlative gift. The birth of a child is associated with hope, uncertainty, joy and also comes with certain challenges. Working back to the very good news of a mother being pregnant, that's where the excitement and fear all begins. The excitement that the woman is going to be a mother is priceless. That does not inhibit the fear of losing the child, the uncertainty of how the child will become and the challenges envisioned that come with raising a child. These are all the intricacies brought about life. Even after the child is grown, the uncertainty and opposition continue to him or her as an adult. In all the stages of existence there appears to be both happiness and challenges. The challenges of a child mostly are felt by the parent, yet as the child matures he or she begins to see her own challenges. Journeys travelled by individuals vary greatly. Some experience more happiness than pain and yet again some experience more pain than happiness in their quest in life. Whatever the case, no one is certain of the journey. Life is given by God whether to human beings, animals or to nature as a whole. Whether there changes brought about some forces to the existence of all these things or not, the fact remains that life was given. Drawing conclusions or assumptions from my very own life and the life of the ones that surround me, I have come to realize that opposition is inevitable. Further that the guiding book given to humanity for direction, correction, reprimand and comfort seem to reveal that in life opposition is guaranteed (1 Peter 4:12, John 10:10, James 4:7, 1 Corinthians 10:13).

Opposition could be in a form of sickness, poverty, evil forces, abuse and many others. With all these opposing factors human beings face, there is surely a solution one way or another. There seem to be a thin line between opposition and challenges. These terms can be used interchangeably to amount to the same conclusion. If one is facing opposition, it means that individual is facing a challenge. Challenges bring about discomfort and anxiety in the life of the one facing such. This book therefore will try and ascertain or discuss some mitigation strategies to opposition. The founding principles of the solutions will be primarily drawn from scripture and also personal encounters. Challenges should not nullify the person, but should be dealt with to find lasting solutions.

CHAPTER 1

DISCOVERING OPPOSITION

For I know the plans I have for you; declares the Lord, plans to prosper you and not to harm you, plans to give you hope and a future (.Jeremiah 29:11).

One of my earliest encounter with opposition was at a very tender age when I was still in Primary school. I was presumable a bright student in class. So I was getting the first position since grade 1 up to standard three. Looking at it now, I realize that I was not necessarily a very bright student per say. The thing that made me appear superior to the other students was the location of the school. This school was in the rural areas and the good teachers normally do not want to teach in the rural areas. If a chance presented itself they will apply for a transfer to the schools in towns. Further that there are other things that contribute to students in the rural areas not performing well. So I would not consider myself a very bright student. However I was an above average student considering the way I was quick to master concepts in class. When I got to standard 3, I started to be very sick and this kind of sickness was not one where you feel pain. It was in a way that my understanding of concepts started declining at an alarming level. I went from getting position 1 to position 14. The teachers couldn't understand and my grandmother also was puzzled. I tried working hard and started studying even though I was not studying before. I would easily master concepts in class and remember them when the examination time came. This time, that was not the case. I had to start studying to remember things and even when the examination approached I remembered little. I started feeling some movement of things in my head. At first I thought it was hair lies and my hair was cut short to prevent the presumed lies infestation. On close examination my grandmother noticed that I had no lies at all. As though that was not enough, I started to lose my hair especially at the back and will spend much of my time scratching my head because I could feel these things moving from my head. Sometimes I would plug out my hair thinking I was removing the things moving in hair. This was very devastating. I remember crying one day when I got my report card. I had again attained position 14 which I was not happy with because I had experience being in the top position for about 5 years. My grandmother quickly realized there was a problem, but couldn't tell what it was. My mother was informed of the problem as she stayed in one of the city centres due to employment and I was staying with my grandmother. So they started to look for solutions.

I remember being taken to various hospitals and the doctors diagnosed different things and gave me medication. Such medication was unhelpful at all. Eventually my mother decided to remove me from that school and moved me to an urban school. The damage had already been done because even in those schools, I went from being above average to being an average student. Realizing that this could be a spiritual battle my grandmother suggested that I should be taken to some traditionalist. That traditionalist confirmed this as a spiritual attack and recommended some herbs which were not that helpful either.

As I look back at that kind of predicament I faced as a child, I realized that challenges are not only for adults. Children also face numerous challenges and sometimes are unable to voice them out. A lot of abuse cases are kept unreported in fear of the damage the assailant promised to do if such cases are disclosed. Such abuse could be from the parents, siblings, neighbors, teachers, family members, and sometimes from the so called friends. Joseph experience pain at a very tender age. At the age of seventeen, his brothers sold him to be slave in a foreign land. They were not fond of him because their father openly loved him more than he love them. He even made an ornate robe for him. He loved Joseph because he had been born to him at an old age (Genesis 37:3). Apart from being favoured by his father, he also appeared to be favoured by God. His peculiar dreams suggested that he was going to be prominent man as compared to his brothers. He dreamt of his brothers and himself binding sheaves of grain out in the field when suddenly his sheaf rose and stood upright, while his brothers sheaves gathered around his and bowed down to it (Genesis 37:5). It indicated the favour upon his life and this infuriated his brothers and they hated him even more. From the very day he was sold, his life was never the same again. He encountered several challenges and also tremendous favour along his journey. In all those challenges he faced the Lord gave him success in everything he did (Genesis 39:3). These hard times increased his trust in God, such that now God had given him the gift of interpreting dreams. This very gift was the very thing that led him to freedom and highest office in Egypt. When going through hard times, always know that the Lord is making a way where it appears to be no way. God never leave his people in shame.

David was also not immune to opposition at a tender age. He found himself being a shepherd of his father's sheep. As the youngest he was the one to be sent to the wilderness to tender his father's sheep. We do not hear of his brother giving him a break sometimes. Being alone in the wilderness is not a nice thing. Often times boys who tender the flock of their fathers, have to do it even when it's raining. In my own experience as well, we had to take care of the flock at home at a very tender age. We had to rush home immediately after school to take care of the livestock. While other children were enjoying riding on their newly acquired bicycles and partake in other childhood thrills we were in the wilderness following the flock. In other homes, even during Christmas day, they have to be out there in the wild while other people are celebrating Christmas. It is a painful thing. David was considered as nothing at all. Taking a closer scrutiny at the wilderness one realizes that it is potentially not a bad place after all. It was while in the wild that David started acquainting himself with the Lord. Being in the wilderness allowed him to experience victories his brothers only dreamt of. He was able to subdue a lion and a bare. This was only a boy, how could he manage to deaf these dangerous beasts. The answer is simple, the hand of the Lord was upon him. This is clearly noticed when he had to face Goliath. He told Goliath that he was coming to him in his (Goliath) own name trusting his own strength, but David assured him that he was coming in the name of God who sustained me in the wilderness (1 Samuel 17:45). He attested to the fact that the reason why he was able to kill those animals was not because of his own strength. His firm stance was that such victory was granted by God. This strongly suggest that victory is guaranteed even to children if they believe in the one who gives them strength (Philippians 4:13). When David saw Goliath, he saw nothing at all. Although to many he appeared as a challenge, he saw him as nothing. This is because he knew the power of the one who was in him. Opposition should not be feared, but faced with the knowledge that the one in us is greater than that challenges. When we put our faith in God, other things become nothing at all.

There appear to be power attracted while in the wilderness (Isaiah 35; 1-10). David drew power in the wilderness. The storms or your wilderness could be a platform for you to draw power. The wilderness is a training ground for giants. When soldiers are trained, sometimes they are taken into the wilderness for training to be able to master the environment so that when they are deployed to fight in the wilderness, they can stand. They would be already familiar with the wilderness and when nothing is disturbing them in wilderness while training, they tend to focus on the training rather than being distracted by the busy environments. So soldier on in the wilderness your training ground and draw power to stand against your adversaries.

Jesus also loved praying out in the wilderness, especially on mountains. A number of miracles happened in the wilderness while He was there. The recording of Matthew draw us into a time when Jesus went to the wilderness after hearing the news of John's death

(Matthew 14:10-12). The people heard of this and they followed Him into the desert place by foot. This moved Jesus and was filled with compassion towards the people. In turn He healed their sick. The scripture suggest that He took some time in the wilderness praying and fellowshipping with the people. Seeing that it was getting late His disciples suggested that He send the people away back to their homes because that was a desert place. Being in such a place for some time also resulted in the people getting hungry (Matthew 14:15). He appeared to enjoy the time spent with the people and thus did not want them to go. Instead he instructed his disciples to feed them. They didn't have enough food to feed everyone. They only had five loaves of bread and two fishes which was enough only for themselves. Jesus instructed them to bring the loaves and fishes to him and looked up to heaven while blessing the food. After breaking the food, he gave it to His disciples to give to the people. To everyone's amazement, the food became sufficient for all and there were even some left-overs (Matthew 14:17). The excess food filled twelve baskets after all five thousand people were full. The food miraculously multiplied and this show how powerful the hand of the Lord is. After taking the food into his hands and blessed it, it became sufficient for all (Matthew 14:20-21).

Another miracle that took place in the wilderness is recorded in the seventh chapter of Matthew. Jesus took Peter, James and John his brother to a high mountain. While in the mountain, He was transfigured before his disciples and His face shone like the sun (Matthew 17:1-4). Scripture posit that His raiment became white as the light. Then in the midst of what was happening, Moses and Elias appeared and were seen conversing with Jesus. Moses and Elias had died a long time before this encounter. Yet when He is transfigured they are seen by the disciples talking with Jesus. As they were watching, they had a loud voice speaking and saying 'This is my beloved Son, in whom I'm well pleased, hear Him' (Matthew 17:5-6). The wilderness is also a place where the devil tried to tempt the Lord. Again the Israelites were sustained in the wilderness. It was place of learning and trusting God. We hear of God opening up the red sea for them so they could cross when their enemies, the Egyptians, were pursuing them (Exodus 14:16). God further went on to bless them with water and manna while in the desert place. The situation appeared dire to the Israelites while in the wilderness. Suddenly they realized they were without food and started complaining to Moses why he removed them from Egypt where they had access to any food they wanted (Exodus 16:3).

As much as the wilderness attracts grace and miracles, but also it brings about uncertainty and fear. These people did not know what they would eat and they thought they would surely die. When we are led into the wilderness, we find ourselves complaining because of the fear of the unknown. It appears that death is looming and there appears to be no solution to the problem. But what the Lord who forces us or allows us to go into the wilderness, He already has a plan for us. It might not be revealed in the beginning of the storm. But in the midst of the storm, there shall God supply our needs according to His riches in glory. The Lord explicitly promised to rain down bread for his people and indeed He did (Exodus 16:4).

The wilderness is a place of worship and exaltation to the Lord. In Exodus (5:1) God instructed Pharaoh to let his people go so they could hold a festival for him in the wilderness. Exodus refers to the wilderness as a place to make sacrifices to the Lord (Exodus, 5:2). It is a perfect place to be with God without interruptions. The people while in Egypt were busy with meaningless things of the world which did not benefit them, but were of benefit to the Egyptians. Going into the wilderness would give them time and chance to focus on God and thus strengthen their knowledge of Him. It is a place of growth and total reliance unto God.

1.1.1 The turning point and victory

It was not until I got to high school that I discovered the gospel. There were Christian services held by the students during lunch breaks and on Fridays after school because we had short times of learning on Fridays. I decided to attend these services and I found that I enjoyed them a great deal. During one of these services I decided to give my life to Christ after one of the students preach drawing his teaching from the book Matthew, *'Come to Me, all you who are weary and burdened, and I will give you rest' (Matthew 11:28).* From henceforth I really developed a zeal to know more about the Lord and participated in prayers and bible classes both in school and at hostel because it was a boarding school. I discovered growth in my walk with the Lord. The sickness was still there and it was getting worse. What I realized was that by joining the church, it appeared to make the sickness worse. Looking at it now reminds me of Gideon when he was visited by an angel. The angel came and sat down under the oak tree at Ophrah that belonged Joash. As Gideon was busy separating wheat from the chaff in a winepress to keep the wheat from the Medianites he saw the angel by the tree. What God revealed to Gideon through the angel puzzled him and he thought he was not the rightful person for the job. He undermined himself and never believe that this was an angel of God. As a result he requested for a sign. The angel of the Lord touched the meat and the bread which Gideon had prepared with the end of the stick which was in his hand. Fire jumped up from the rock and completely burned up the meat and the bread. This made him realize that indeed he had seen an angel of God (Judges 6:11-23). This changed his perspective on things. I discovered that discovering what the opposing spirit is and discovering something greater than your own knowledge and also greater than the opposing spirit coerces change. Although the angel in Gideon case was not an opposing spirit, but it was a discovery of a superior spirit or superior power. Discovering a superior power leads to transformation. Whether that transformation is positive or negative is another thing. I believe Gideon's encounter with the angel of the Lord brought positive transformation in his life. If you put sugar in a cup of tea, that sugar might not fully dissolve if you don't steer the tea. By steering the tea, the sugar completely dissolves and makes the tea sweet that you may be able to enjoy it.

The other prominent observation I picked up was that sometimes change does not come instantly. The discovery opens a channel for things to beginning to change. Paul's encounter with the Lord brought about change (Acts 26:12-19). I believe His total transformation happened over time. Over time he began to solicit information about the things of the Lord and he grew in his belief in God. This was a man who was totally against the people of God and was rampant in killing them. Yet when he discovered someone greater than himself, his actions changed. In his imagination, he was superior to the people and his actions also suggested that he thought himself superior than their God. This lame idea of his was brought crumbling down when he discovered the owner of the people. God always rain supreme in whatever situation. Similarly Goliath thought he was thee man when it came to terrorizing God's people. He feared no man and ultimately did not fear their God. To prove His supremacy God sent a boy to nullify a giant in his own eyes (1 Samuel 17:41-50). The scripture reveals that Goliath had brought fear to the people of God for years. Every time he appeared, their mouths were shut. They thought they had no solution to this giant. This is not because God did not see what Goliath was doing. I believe also that the people were constantly praying for God to remove this reproach from their lives. Yet for years God seemed quiet. The discovery I made about this story was that God acts in His own time. We cannot push God to do what we want. He does things His own way and at His own time. While this man was bullying God's people, He was busy training a young soldier to bring shame to Goliath. When David was ready, God placed him at the right place at the right time. As discussed in the upper section of this book, in 1 Samuel 17:28 we see that David was despised especially by his brothers and was only seen as a shepherd only worthy to take care of their father's sheep. At the right time God exposed His power planted deep inside David. Numerous times in our walk with God, we feel like we are nothing and all alone sometimes. Forgetting that in those very dark times of our lives, He is constantly orchestrating ways to rescue us.

 If we keep our eyes focused on him in prayer and supplication, eventually that mountain we are facing will collapse (Psalm 34:5-7, Hebrews 12:2, Isaiah 26:3). He promises us perfect peace and also if we call on him, he promises to answer and show us great and might things which we do not know (Jeremiah 33:3). Many are times when people elevate themselves and give themselves titles less deserved. Even situations or problems sometimes present themselves as superior in our lives. But when our owner arrives or decides to act, that self-elevation becomes nothing at all.

Reverting back to the sickness that was in my life, I realized that by giving my life to Christ, the spirits were angry and thus intensified the fight. This was the reason why it appeared to me as if the sickness was getting worse. By giving my life to Christ made these spirits to start to act differently. The sighting I made was that this thing on my head would move to the back of my neck when I was in church. When it was on my neck I would feel heaviness in my neck but there would be no movement in my hair. After the service, the itching in my head will appear again. Additionally every time I prayed, I would feel this thing leaving my head going down to my neck and sometimes to my back. It was then that I concluded that this was a spiritual battle. This discovery made me focus more on the things of the Lord, reading scripture, praying and I even joined the choir. This made me very happy in my spirit. My marks in class were still average and every time this thing was in my head, I couldn't think straight. It was attacking my memory and my ability to master theories in class. By distracting my concentration in class, the spirits had concluded that I would surely fail. I persevered in studying hard and praying always. The

Lord was assuredly with me in my struggle because I passed well in my junior secondary examinations. Every time I felt this attack I would pray and then my mind would clear and would remember what I had studied. The tendency of this spirit was to attack more especially when it was time for writing examinations. I remember every time we were instructed to begin the exams, it would confuse my mind and I would focus on scratching my head instead of writing. I knew that I was under attacked every time it appeared. So the Lord taught me to pray in my heart without opening my mouth. I would call upon the name of the Lord Jesus in silence.

After sometime the spirit would leave me or I would feel something moving to my back. It was not painful at all. When the spirit left, my concentration would return and the itching would be better. I would discover that about 10 minutes or more of examination time had elapse already. My focus would be then on the things I knew in trying to race against time. I recall vividly that I passed very well both in my junior secondary and high school obtaining first classes. In my high school years, I was getting stronger in the Lord and that's why my prayer life grew. This was the reason I passed well.

I therefore know for sure the hand of the Lord is active. An encounter with the Lord for me began in those early years and this led into my faith in God getting stronger. At university level the spirit was still there yet my spiritual life had evolved. It just wouldn't leave me. It was suppressed when I prayed, but never completely left my life. My discovery was that some spirits are stubborn and now I understand clearly the scriptures when the Lord instructs us to pray without ceasing (1 Thessalonians 5:17-19). The spirit world is a complicated world we can never fully fathom. We are indeed not fighting against flesh and blood, but against principalities. Principalities can never be won by acting important in the presence of the Lord. They teach you how to be a warrior in the spirit. While evil forces perceive to have conquered you, Jehovah is laughing and granting you victories you can never imagine. The more I was attacked, it appeared to be a platform for elevation for me.

The annals of Exodus divulge a profound happenstance in Egypt. The king Pharaoh had enslaved the people of Israel of the premise that they had become numerous for the Egyptians. *So they put slave masters over them, with forced labor and they build Pithome and Rameses as store cities for Pharoah (Exodus 1:11).* This was the beginning of slavery for the Israelites. A very challenging and degrading era in their lives which would last for years. This is something they never anticipated. These were the people of God, yet the Lord allowed this to last for years. Yet when the time was right He rescued them through the hand Moses. The profound thing I noticed in the writings of Exodus was that the more the people of God were attacked, the more they grew. This further annoyed the Egyptians and they oppressed them even more, working them ruthlessly (Exodus 1:12). The conclusion I made was that opposition is just a mechanism that attacks victory. The enemy may think, he is winning by oppressing you, but the reality is that the victory always is the Lords. Some of the smart students I attending high school with never made it to university and some had to upgrade their studies in order to qualify for university. For me, it was the hand of the Lord that ushered me straight to university.

1.2 Discovering opposition in the bible models

Upon hearing the news that the Ammonites, Mobites and Mount Seir were on their way to wedge war against king Jehoshaphat, he was chockfull with fear. One would have thought that the first thing a king who was familiar with war, would summon all the armies and instruct them to get ready for war. On the contrary he decided to do something peculiar and an honorable thing. He tore up his clothes and called a fast across all Judah. Clearly a man who knew the power of God and respected His guidance rather than seeking men's strategies on how to deal with the threat. He seeked counsel from the one who created it all. His discovery was that this approaching army was potentially strong than they were. This discovery made him seek counsel from the one who was strong than the approaching army (2 Chronicles 20:1-11). I have observed amongst some of the people I know that when they face challenges, the first reference point is to a therapist or hospital or even a traditionalist. People seem to undermine the authority of God. They view another person as the solution to their problems. Once they have failed in their primary sources of help, it is then that they decide to seek the services of a Pastor who can commune with God pertaining the matter. There seem to be some kind of blindness in the eyes of many. No wonder the records in Corinthians clearly state that the god of this world has blinded the minds of the unbelievers, to keep them from seeing the light of the gospel of the glory of Christ who is the image of God (1 Corinthians 4:4).

For Jehoshaphat, the first reference point was to God. As they fasted and prayed while the army was on their way to attacked them, the word of the Lord came through the prophet of God Jahaziel. There were clear instructions and assurance that victory shall be theirs. God provided assurance, confidence and comfort to His people (2 Chronicles 20:14-17). If the king Jehoshaphat had handled the matter his own way, surely the outcome could have be something else. Discovering opposition humbles you and reminds you that you are only human. It makes you forget your position of authority and sick counsel from the supreme authority which is God. Relying on your own capabilities or abilities could result in calamitous consequences.

What we think will bring solutions can sometimes be the very thing that lead us to opposition. Looking at the story of Hagar in the archives of Genesis, that possibility becomes eminent. Abram and Sarai were husband and wife for a very long time. In their union however no child was conceived. This brought pain particularly to Sarai, who then suggested that her husband go in unto Hagar their servant. She would have loved to have her own children. But looking at her age and that of her husband, they concluded that it would never happen. They had accepted their fate which was primarily the reason for Sarai to recommend Hagar to her husband. Her plan was to treat Hagar's children as her own (Genesis 16:2). Sarai never thought that her suggestion would bring more pain than comfort. Hagar conceived of Abram and the immediate thing she opted to do was to despise Sarai her mistress. This never went down well with Sarai. In chapter sixteen of Genesis and the fifth verse Sarai was clearly voicing out her grief to her husband because of the way her servant was ill-treating her. The actions of Abram after hearing her wife's concerns were proof of his commitment to his wife. Whether they had children or not, he was still honoring his wife. He told her to deal with Hagar whichever way was pleasing to her (Genesis 16:6). What Sarai assumed was a solution had all of sudden become a challenge. Opposition creeps into our lives unnoticed and sometimes our noble actions can open doors for it to strike. Strange how people attack the ones who helped them at some point in their lives. Finding yourself loathed by someone you thought should be thanking you compels pain beyond measure.

In the midst of her pain Sarai began to retaliate by mistreating Hagar basing her actions from what her husband had told her. Seeing that she was not getting much support from Abram, Hagar opted to leave. Scripture states that as she was fleeing from her mistress, an angel of the Lord appeared to her and inculcated her to return back to Sarai and submit to her as her mistress (Genesis 16:9). Looking at this happenstance, one realizes that God has his own ways of repaying us for our pain. What derides you or appear to be a problem, the Lord will cause it to submit to you just as He did with Hagar. The enemy may think he got you down and flat, but the Lord shall surely cause the opposition to turn around and become a blessing to you. God is so merciful and just to forgive our wrong doings. Hagar was forgiven as a result of her obedience to God. Her obedience also caused the Lord to bless her with more children.

The detested are promised victory in numerous scriptures in the Bible (Psalm46:10; Isaiah 43:1-2:1, Peter 5:10, Psalm 9:9-19). For Sarai, victory eventually came because God remembered them in their old age. The Lord blessed them with a son even though they had passed their child bearing stage (Genesis 17:15). The book of Genesis discloses that the promise of a child also brought about alteration to their names. Sarai became Sarah and Abram became Abraham. This leads to the inference that their present names could not be able to carry the magnitude of the promise the Lord was planting in their lives. When God nullifies the opposition in a life of a person, he also gives the person different status. How people look at you and address you changes. You are addressed as an overcomer instead of a failure. The newly acquired status also bring absolute respect. Trusting Him in dire situations where it appears to be no way has the benefit of attracting absolute joy when the storm ends (Isaiah 43:16; Isaiah 43:18-19). According to Gordon (2022) following the designed path for your life does not guarantee that you shall not pass through waters and challenges. Her article submits that facing opposition is a sign that God desires to use you to help others. In order to render perfect support to others, you must have gone through a similar situation yourself. God always makes a way for the oppressed, but sometimes He allows them to go through the storm so that His power may be publicized. You cannot bypass a storm that has to bring power in your life. He allows you to go through it and sustains you while going through.

The woman with an issue of blood was greatly despised by many as a consequence of her condition. Her encounter with Jesus altered her status. She was probably being called by the sickness instead of her real name. But the encounter with the Lord brought absolute healing. She discovered how nice being without infirmity was. Furthermore she discovered that there is healing in Jesus. Just by touching the helm of His garment, she was made whole (Luke 8:43-48). Scripture posit that she had spent everything she had consulting different physicians in pursuit of healing. She disbursed all she heard on trying to acquire help, but it never came. This is a woman who had been sick for 12 years. This is a long time of pain and suffering, yet when she discovered Jesus, her faith compelled her to touch the helm of His garment. Instantly what she had spent everything trying to cure diminished. Discovering and acknowledging that you have a problem induces you to seek help. This women never locked herself up in her house, but instead went about looking for a solution. Hiding from society because of a challenge you going through will not erase the challenge. Constantly knocking and seeking help, is bound to bring a solution to that challenge (John 15:16, John 14:13).

The blind man who sat by the road side begging, discovered that something unusual was happening through the noise he heard. On enquiry, he learnt that Jesus was passing by. Instantly he lifted up his voice and called upon Jesus to have mercy on him. Even though some people were instructing him to be quiet. He never stop calling on Jesus. Upon hearing him, Jesus instructed them to bring the man to him. Jesus asked him what he could do for him. His immediate response was that he wanted to see. Jesus then healed him. The words Jesus spoke are profound because, He attributed the man's healing to his faith. It was the man's faith in Jesus that brought about the healing (Luke 18:35-43, James 1:6, 1John 5:15). He discovered something bigger than the blindness and acted by calling unto the one greater. It was the calling on Jesus and his faith that conveyed his healing. When we call upon the Lord he promises to answer and tell us great things which we do not know (Jeremiah 33:3). Opposition then should teach us to call upon the one who promised never leave us no forsake us. He instructs us not be terrified in whatever situation we may find ourselves in (Deuteronomy 31:6, Joshua 1:9, Chronicles 28:20).

The death of Lazarus brought pain to his family members. When he was brought back to life by Jesus, they were overwhelm with joy. The power of God can be seen through these instances mentioned above. God has no limits and there is nothing too hard for Him. Clearly there is nothing impossible with God (Luke 1:37). A man who had been dead for a number of days and was even buried is restored back to life. When Jesus arrived, he spoke life to the lifeless body and Lazarus was restored to life (John 11:38). The power to bring back life cannot be paralleled with anything. After all life belongs to God and thus He can give it or take it at any time he pleases.

Hannah and Peninnah's records in scripture bears similar attributes to that of Sarah and Hagar. The book of 1 Samuel begins with a story of Elkanah who had two wives Hannah and Peninnah. In the narrative of the story, it is portrayed that Peninnah had children and Hannah was unable to conceive. In discovering her opposition, Peninnah started to harass Hannah just to aggravate her. Her childlessness had become something to vex her continuously and cause her pain (1Samuel 6:6-9). According to Kadari (1999) Peninnah would purposely infuriate Hannah in a roundabout manner, so that she could not be directly charged with improper behavior by their husband, while hurting her rival. Hannah discovered that her rivalry had become a problem and decided to act. Her actions were not to attack Peninnah directly, but her attack was through prayer. She kept on seeking the face of God in tears. One of the days while she was praying in her heart Eli the priest noticed her. Her lips were seen moving, but no sound was heard and Eli thought she was drunk. On confronting her, Eli discovered that she was in distress. He spoke a blessing upon her life and told her to go in peace. Not long thereafter, a miracle occurred in

Hannah's life and she conceived. God blessed her with a son (1 Samuel 1:20). That was not the only miracle she received. Further on in chapter 2 of the book of Samuel, it is publicized that the Lord was gracious to her and she also gave birth to 3 sons and two daughters (1 Samuel 2:21). Through her constant praying and asking the Lord for help, she received her miracle. The Lord rewards those who diligently seek Him and also the Lord has a way to avenge those who are persecuted (Hebrews 11:6).

1.3 Positioning yourself to overcome

Overcoming requires a certain attitude and mindset. The refusal spirit should be incarnated in us knowing that we are not alone, but Christ leaves in us. We should refuse to be defeated and have absolute faith that the situation will change. The scripture in the book of Philippians (4:13) states that I can do all things through Christ who strengthens me. Such knowledge is a power pill. Knowledge of who you are in Christ should be your driving force in dealing with opposition. You may not know how to handle the situation, but giving it all unto the Lord removes you from being burdened by the situation. It gives you peace of mind while in pain.

In all his gruesome opposition Paul seemed to shift the focus from himself and instead engrossed on the work of God. The opposition was never a barrier to the work. Through all his trials he never lost focus. It would seem the challenges made him stronger in his walk with the Lord. He even recorded in Galatians affirming that he had realized that he no longer took value of his own life but immersed himself in the affairs of God the everlasting father. He realized that focusing on himself was all vanity, but focusing on the superior undertakings of God produced greater rewards (Galatians 2:20). When our focus is shifted from the challenge, God guarantees us victory. The challenge should not remove us from the things of God and the knowledge of His love. Instead should draw us closer to Him. As we take time to dwell on His promises, then He takes the time to focus on our affairs (Mathew 6:33). For Paul this information had recessed deep down into his heart such that he never took time to worry much about little things. He appeared to be concerned about spreading the good news of the gospel and also helping others grow in faith. While doing that he attained a lot of rewards. While incarcerated, Paul and Silas focused on the Lord instead of worrying about their situation. This led to realizing one of the greatest miracle that was not known to people. It is uncommon for prison doors to open by themselves. In actual fact this puzzled the jailor to such an extent that he wanted to end his own life. This was indeed what men thought was impossible forgetting that all things are possible to those who believe (Mark 9:23). The miracle was realized solely because they removed themselves from the problem and focused on worshipping God. It was common for them to reverence the Father even when the times were not conducive. The wonder therefore is why people fail to emulate such behavior. God's love is unconditional, wholehearted and continual. Nothing a man can do to expand God's love and absolutely nothing to make Him love less (Chapel, 2022).

Worrying over what we cannot control is potentially a waste of time and energy. Our focus should be on worship in the midst of opposition just like these great men of valor. While it appeared like their condition was permanent, they shifted their eyes away from the predicament and concentrated on the one who held their future. Once you realize that God is the one who holds your future and also grasp that nothing is impossible with Him, that knowledge brings confidence in struggle. Such firm assurance that one way or the other you will overcome.

My struggle in finding employment was paralyzing. After I completed my Master's degree, I thought I was going to be easy to get a job. After all statistics were saying there was a shortage of postgraduate candidates with experience. With my previous exposure in the work environment coupled with my qualifications, I thought I was set. So I ventured into applying for several positions hoping that I would be offered different positions so I could choose what I liked or what was better paying and with the prospects of expanding my territories. To my dismay, I was not even being shortlisted for any of the positions I had applied for. I continued to apply, and marketed myself to the ones I thought were in my corner, my connection and friends. What happened was utterly confusing. Instead of helping me, it appeared as if they were the ones sabotaging my efforts of getting employed. A certain man called me and warned me of my references. I had put names of previous bosses and friends as references. I was completely shuttered when I heard the news that some of the friends never had anything good to say about me when they were contacted as references. Mind you these were people whom I had supported when they faced challenges. With this new found information I opted to modify my curriculum vitae and changed the references. Years and years elapsed and still there was nothing. A lot of the companies I applied to never even responded to acknowledge my application, let alone to inform me I was not shortlisted. By now I was getting really frustrated and confused. Was I really not qualifying or was there a spirit behind? I started to strongly seek the face of God. To my dismay it appeared as though God was quiet or not hearing my prayers. Was I doing anything wrong I thought? There was no one to respond to that question either. My life was filled with bitterness. Every day I applied for several positions with no luck. This even reminded me of David's pain in the book of Psalm 38. David was like giving a petition to God when he said '*O Lord, do not rebuke me in your anger or discipline me in your wrath. For your arrows have pierce me and your hand has come down upon me (Psalm 38:1-6)*. I really felt very low and all day I was mourning just like David.

The friends I had stopped calling me and some even blocked my number. It was like people were laughing at me instead of helping me. I even reported the matter to the church especially in the men's committee to help if they heard of any job openings, but you can tell when people only agree with their mouths. By now I had no money to even go to church sometimes. No one even bothered to check on me even from the church members' or so called friends. The ones who called were only calling to laugh or mock me. My pastor prayed for me when I reported the matter to him. I literally went everywhere to find help but nothing came. This was really the toughest days of my life. In all this pain, the Lord never forgot about me. The queen of my life was always by my side supporting me both financially and spiritually. I have never met such a selfless woman. She went all out to ensure that I was alright. In the midst of all this darkness, I learnt that the Lord sustains his people no matter what. When He sustains us, the people shall know it and it is not about what we have or who we know. It becomes all about His loving hand. I can safety say the hand of the Lord kept me and I am still standing. All I did in this situation was to position myself in prayer and fasting. The Lord never left me and indeed was awesome in my pain. Positioning yourself for success in such hard times helps retain your sanity.

CHAPTER 2

HIS GRACE IS SUFFICIENT.

My grace is sufficient for you, for power is made perfect in weakness (2 Corinthians 12:9)

For me his grace has always been more than sufficient. With all the opposition I faced in life, I can attest that if it wasn't for the Lord I would not have made it past 40 years or even 30 years. My challenges weren't just school related although I realized that the attacks were primarily targeting my academic life. Later I would comprehend that by attacking my academic life, the evil forces were trying to render me useless in life. Not until later in my journey did I face similar opposition to the one I faced in high school. Now I was enrolled to pursue my Master's degree. The exhilaration I felt when I got the news that I had been accepted into the Masters programme cannot be explained. It was something I always wanted to do. I realized that I derive pleasure in studying. Throughout my life, I found myself studying something whether enrolled in a short course or something. I am just passionate about attaining information. Later on I even developed the passion for research. So I am always busy with studying, researching or trying to write some article. From the onset of the programme there appeared to be some challenges. I registered and paid the registration fees and was ready to begin my studies. Two months down the line, I realized that there was nothing really happening with my studies. They had sent me all the acceptance letter and information on the structure of the Masters.

On contacting the university I was informed that there was a shortage of supervisors in my field. They however promised to sort this matter out and would notify me once the supervisor had been allocated. That information of assurance uplifted my spirit. At least I knew then that I was not forgotten. This was a research based Master's degree and I was to do it off campus. The only time I had to go to campus was to see the supervisor or to attend seminars organized by the institution. So I continued to wait impatiently for that email or phone call authorizing a supervisor for my studies. I just couldn't wait to begin my studies and the excitement was just too much. Six months down the line, there was still no contact from the university. I couldn't wait any longer, so I opted to contact the university. To my disenchantment I was told that there was still no supervisor allocated for my thesis. I was however invited for a seminar that dealt with qualitative and qualitative data analysis in research. The seminar was an eye opener and quite a number of Masters and Doctorate students were present and it was nice to middle with the other fellow students. That's where I discovered that I was not the only one without a supervisor. The head of the faculty apologized to all of us for the delay in allocating supervisors and then he suggested that we try to approach potential supervisors we think can be able to mentor us. This could be someone within the same institution or from another institution.

With such information, I couldn't waste any more time. Straight away I started searching for a suitable supervisor obviously who was also available to supervise. My first search was perceptibly to look at the lecturers in the same University. After identifying a few I thought were relevant, I sent emails requesting them to supervise my work. A number of them told me that they had the maximum number of students to supervise in one year. Apparently a supervisor was only allowed to supervise a certain number of students per year. Some did not even bother to respond to my emails. Jubilation came one day when I got an email from one potential supervisor, who showed interest in supervising my studies. I contacted him, and we met to discuss a way forward. He submitted his name to management as a willing supervisor and was approved. So my journey began and we started straight away with polishing the thesis proposal. Considering that six months had already elapsed, he tried his level best to push so that we could cover the time lost. We worked hard together and I was pleased with his supervisory skills. He even assisted me in getting a scholarship for my studies. The second challenge that made me realized that there were some evil forces which seemed to be opposing my studies came when I applied for permission to conduct the research to the authorities of the study area. My topic was not really a sensitive one and all it required was to go around the area interviewing random people. It was the kind of research you could just go around the area collecting data from individuals who agreed to answer my questionnaire. But research ethics do not permit such. I was told to submit the proposal to the study area authorities. Two months down the line when I called, they said they were still reading the proposal. So I waited again for another month. When I contacted them again, I was told it has been referred to the headquarters. That gave me an assurance that at least there was progress. Another month down the line still no communication from them. I opted to go to their offices to find out what the delay was about. When I got there I discovered that no one had really read the proposal. They were asking me what the research was about, when did I send the proposal to them, and was told to resend the proposal. Mind you I had lost six months trying to get a supervisor and now another six months of trying to get clearance. I thought to myself there must be some kind of opposition. My fellow students were progressing well and they were far ahead of me.

No one understood why my clearance letter was taking so long. Even the supervisor tried to contact the authorities of the study area and was promised that we would get the clearance in two days. Two days became weeks and weeks became months. I went to their offices again one day and asked to speak to the manager of another department. She agreed to see me and when I explained to her about the research I intended to do, she couldn't understand why I was not cleared. By God's grace she wrote the clearance letter there and then and promised to give me any resources I needed from them. A letter that required less that 5 minutes to write, took six months. This was beyond reading a proposal, but was opposition indeed. I could literally tell that God was now intervening.

So we were back on track and things were really going well until I heard that my supervisor had resigned and could no longer be part of my studies. I was shuttered to say the least. At least his resignation came after we had made major strides with the studies and got the measure approvals necessary to complete the programme. So I had to wait for an allocation of a replacement supervisor. Another six months elapsed before I received the news that my project has been assigned to a new supervisor. For some reason this new supervisor was quiet and never bothered to contact me. There had been too much time wasted on my studies so, I decided to contact her seeing that two weeks had passed and there was no correspondence from her. I was relieved when she sounded happy that I called. We arranged to meet and the studies resumed again. My jubilation was cut short when I realized that she wanted us to revert and fixed some things which the previous had approved. It was like we were working backwards instead of moving forward. But at least something was happening. Just when I thought things were starting to move, I hit a snag again. Apparently there were issues on how we had obtained the scholarship. So there were investigations on how the money was obtained and how some of it was spent. That went on for about four months. The studies were halted again due to that investigation. That was the point I gave up on my studies. I had fought too much, and was not ready for any other antagonism. I concluded that the university was really against my studies, but later on I realized this was some evil forces trying to nullify my efforts. There was no communication from the institution for a while after that investigation. I thought they had cancelled everything. I also never bothered to contact them. I had accepted defeat. I was seriously depressed and there was a very close friend of mine who seemed to be interested in how my studies were going. When I elaborated to her about everything that had happened, Ms. Dunn, told me that there was nothing bigger than God. So she encouraged me to pray and she was also praying for me. Sometimes she would come to my place and we prayed together. A firm believer in God. She even suggested we go see some prophets of God of which we did. But my spirit was down through that process. To be honest my faith was a little down and was mostly reliant on her faith. So we waited on God and indeed God came through. Indeed his promises are yes and amen (2 Corinthians 1:20). To sum it all up, my studies were eventually completed and we even published a paper in one of the social sciences journal. Our struggle is not against flesh and blood, but against the rulers, against the powers, against the world forces of this darkness, against the spiritual force of wickedness in the heavenly places (Ephisians 6:12).

2.2 The ones who were with us, but never with us

A storm is a very scary and is a portent that brings fear to people. It is rough and no one really knows when it will come to an end once it starts. Thunder and lightning accompanies it and that large sound of the thunder gets even the toughest man fearful. It has the potential to cause damage to our material possessions and can even claim lives. Some people even hide under tables or something and cover mirrors, shiny things to try and prevent the lightning from striking. My grandfather used to go outside and throw granules of salt in the air when there was a storm. He would instruct the storm to go somewhere else. When I asked him about the purpose of his actions, his response was that sometimes witches send storms to bring destruction to the people who are supposedly their enemies. A phenomenon I would later believe as I grew older. People would testify in church of how the Lord protected them from storms which appeared to be targeting them. Evil spirits would also manifest as the Pastor prayed for congregates and the evil spirits would narrate how they were trying to kill the person by sending a storm. This would be the witch speaking through the possessed individual's voice. Some would even disclosed who they were or where the powers were solicited from. Somehow witches have such powers to create storms and lead them to unsuspecting individuals. We see the power of sorcerous in the chronicles of Exodus. When God instructed Moses and Aaron to perform a miracle in front of king Pharaoh; the instruction was specifically for Moses to tell Aaron to throw down his staff in front of Pharaoh and it would become a snake. Pharaoh called all magicians and sorcerous to come down to where they were. The magicians and sorcerous also performed the same miracle. They also threw down their staffs and they became snakes. The greatest miracle that transpired in this whole situation was when Aaron's snake consumed all the other snakes. These entities have the ability to create illicit things (Exodus 7:8-12, 22; 8:7). The world is full of evil. We are indeed not fighting against flesh and blood, but against principalities as earlier stated (Ephisians 6:12).

When we face storms in a form of opposition in our lives, some come with large sounds and scary gestures which bring uncertainty and fear. It is a time of testing and validation of the individual's faith. Faith as recorded in the book Hebrews is the substance of things hoped for and an assurance of things not seen (Hebrew 11:1). When that faith is tried and tested, the least thing you can expect is help and support from friends, family members and the church, but most of all from God. Sometimes that help seems to be a distant thing that you yearn for so desperately. Instead of helping you, often times people don't but watch and laugh at a distance. Your life becomes the latest news to the ones who know you and whom you expect to be in your corner. That's the time you really know who your real friends are. It's not everyone who will stick around on your dark days. You start to see those who were with you but really not with you. These are like vipers sucking your life dry. You thought they were friends, but all they really were was enemies hoping for your downfall. Real pain incursions when you experience neglect even from family members. Who then do you trust? When the situation you are facing presents to you a bad report, do you believe that report? There is a report that supersedes any other which we are promised by God. Whose report are you going to believe? Trusting people is trusting nothing at all. But putting your trust in the Lord produces victory. The ones you are celebrating your life with right now are potentially not fully in your spade. Joseph trusted his brothers because they were family. He never thought they would one day be the ones to sell him out. He found himself tied down in life as a result of the ones he trusted (Genesis 37:12-36). Peter denied Jesus when times were a little rough. This was a man who had been with Jesus and saw the miracles he performed yet when the storm hit, he disassociated himself from Christ (Luke 22:34, Matthew 26:33-35, Mark 14:29-31). Sometimes the people we value the most run away from us when we are in tempests. Some may run away because they don't know how to help you. But help doesn't have to be money or material things.

Prayer is the greatest support one can ever need when in trials. Why then do they leave when there is something they can offer for free? The inference then becomes that they were never really with you to begin with. In all that running away from your life, learn to release them and hold no grudges. If they can leave you in pain they are not really with you and thus not worthy of shedding a tear over. Learn to lean on Christ the hope of glory and lean not on your own understanding (Proverbs 3:5-6). Putting your trust in people will bring painful surprises. Even though there are people around you now, love them, but not fully give your trust to them. Trust the never changing immortal God.

2.3 The pain of Power

Sometimes pain is associated with power. The power of God conveys comfort but sometimes may lead to solitude. Often times when you are called into some sort of ministry in the gospel you are bound to encounter problems one way or another. This is another space where opposition is rife. While conversing with one man of God, he disclosed to me some of the challenges he encountered in ministry and in his life in general. I would have thought that with all the people surrounding him he would never experience loneliness. To my utter dismay, he pointed out that he sometimes feels secluded and wished to enjoy life like other people. The challenge he mentioned was that as a Pastor people are always watching your life. They expect nothing but perfection all the time. The way you dress, the way you smile, the way you dialogue with other people and who you are talking with. As strange as that may sound, but its reality. When you are seen talking to a woman in town especially to a woman who is deemed by society as a bad or accused of sleeping around with men. They conclude that you are cheating on your wife. The man of God divulged to me that he once met this lady he attended school with and they started talking, discussing about their days in school and also their current lives. Some believer spotted them and began to spread unfounded news that he associated with doggy women and that meant he was cheating. When he heard the news he was devastated especially because one way or another his image was destroyed. How was he to know that the woman had become doggy? 'Even if he knew why didn't people think I was ministering to her instead of jumping into unsubstantiated conclusions? I had no answer to his question. That's the pain of being a minister of the gospel. 'Better still the woman could have been my neighbor so we were just talking as neighbors. Just because I'm pastoring a church does not mean I can't talk to my unsaved neighbors. How will I win them to Christ if I don't talk to them?" He asked. The journey of ministering the gospel does not come easy, but reliance on the one who called you will surely sustain your call and make you find comfort in Him and yourself.

Job experienced such excruciating pain when he lost all his valuable possessions. Apart from losing material things, he also lost his precious children. What a tragedy and pain of losing everything in such a short space of time. The expected thing was to get support from the closet people in his life. This was a prominent person who was respected and had employed a number of people. A lot of people benefitted from his riches. Yet when the storm hit, it appeared that many abandoned him. He got rejection even from his wife. For the wife to utter such discouraging words was bizarre for a woman who had seen the hand of the Lord upon Job his husband. She told him to curse his God and die (Job 2:1-9). This suggests that she had given up on him. Above it all her utterance points to the fact that she had lost her faith in God. How can the one who vowed to be with you in sickness and in health turn around to be the discouraging one. It's a strange thing, but proves that not everyone is really with you. This season was a time of validation and promotion in his life. Such promotion came in a form of opposition. Little did anyone know that this was opposition allowed by God the King of kings? This case of Job show that we shouldn't always ascribe opposition to the devil. Some challenges are nothing but a channel to the next level. Had Job done what his wife was suggesting, he would have ultimately lost his life and missed out on the promotion. He stood firmly in his belief in God. Through him not rejecting God, he got only what others dream of having. It's not that he was not in pain or had some kind of fear. We blatantly hear his distress in the recording of Job (15:24). He even cursed the day he was born (Job 3:1). In all his complaining and uncertainty, he kept his faith intact. When we lose the ones we love and trust, let us not lose our faith in God also. Firmly affirming your faith in hard times has magnitude rewards.

As an Agricultural expect I ponder how seeds are planted into the soil and allowed to rot. Seeds are planted in the ground potentially with manure. The manure is a catalyst for growth. It provides a conducive environment for the seed to produce the plant. As the seed rots underground where no one can see, it begins to germinate. The germination process itself is a miracle. As it dies it produces more of itself. What was buried begins to sprout and a shoot becomes visible. It protrudes above the soil. What happens first is that the seed produces a taproot. That primary root goes down deep into the soil and acts as an anchor for the shoot which protrudes above the ground. Other roots stem out from the primary root to further provide strength to the growing crop. The plant grows and matures and thus produces more seeds. The product of the plant becomes food and also becomes seed to be planted again and obtain more plants. I assessed opposition in light of the mechanics involved in the plant cycle. Firstly I realized that the seed has to be planted before it can die to give rise to the plant. In storms life becomes like we are being planted. As the storms and pain intensify, it is a stage where the old seed is dying to give room to the new. You cannot pour new wine into an old wine skin (Mark 2:22). Later after the storm, the comprehension is that life becomes better and an envy to others. This is because when the plant has produced and is ready for harvest, many start to be interest in the product. Very few would be interested in the crop while it is still at its growth stage. When therefore storms are encountered they should be considered as the breathing ground for new life. A life that will not only benefit the affected, but also others. The people who look down upon you in your darkness may not realize that the storm you went through would benefit them also one way or another. As the lord promotes you into higher dimensions and puts you in a prominent office, the benefits are countless. Count it all joy when you are being persecuted (1 John 3:16-18)

CHAPTER 3

THE POWER OF THE CROSS

And He Himself bore our sins in His body on the cross so that we might die to sin and live to righteousness by His wounds we are healed (1 Peter 2:24)

Jesus' journey to the cross was not an easy one and I doubt if there is any man alive who can voluntarily agree to be immersed in such agonizing pain and embarrassment that Jesus went through. He always knew this time would come and that was the whole purpose of His coming to the world. He suffered and endured the cross to rescue his people from sin and oppression. His death brought to us life eternal and above it all victory over every situation (1 Corinthians 15:55, 2 Corinthians 5:1, Romans 8:1-3). Bergel (2019) states that Christ's death on the cross is offered as the pivotal point of Apocalypse's vision, and the goal is to concede God's rule on earth as it is already recognized in heaven. His work while citing Du Rand (2005) posit that the death on the cross is an accomplishment, which consists of all the works done by the Lamb to procure salvation to humanity, and the consequences, which concentrate on describing God's and Lamb's actions to appropriate the salvation to the whole world. The primary reason for his crucifixion was to redeem his people from sin and allow them to have a free gift of salvation. No one goes to the father but through Christ (John 14:6). Jesus is presented in scripture as the only way to gain access to the Father. He is the way the truth and the life. In Him there is life. It means if we really desire true life, we need to acquaint ourselves with the Son. His dying on the cross was a way of paying a price for our sins, so that we can no longer perish, but have eternal life (John 10:28). In order to have that everlasting life, we ought to accept the Lord Jesus as our Lord and Saviour and turn away from ours sins in repentance (Revelation 2:6). To repent is similar to apologizing for the wrongs you have done. But repentance has to be followed by turning away from the sins. You ask for forgiveness and then get rid of the sin you are apologizing for. Giving your life to Christ gives you light. You begin to live in the light knowing the good deed of the Lord and the whole purpose of existence (Romans 13:12, 1 John 2:9, Ephesians 5:11).

Though it may appear like we are struggling in this world, everlasting life is promised to us in heaven. God shall wipe away all our tears from our eyes when he comes for his people. There will be no more death or mourning or crying or pain for those who rest on Him. The old order of the things would have passed away (Revelation 21:4). Just because of the cross, our hearts remain strong and courageous while we await his return (Psalm 31:24). Waiting upon the Lord is a good thing. It may appear that the waiting comes with many challenges, but Isaiah recorded an assurance that, they that wait upon the Lord shall renew their strength. They shall mount up with wings as eagles; they shall run and not be wary; they shall walk and not faith (Isaiah 40:31). This is such an awesome promise. The benefits of waiting upon the Lord are a spectacle to many. They wonder how the persecuted are still standing firm in their belief in God. All kinds of storms had hit them, yet they still proclaim His Majesty. The journey is not about us, but the whole purpose of existence is so that God can be glorified.

Through the cross, the Lord made us victorious. He gave us salvation by giving his life to death. We are now redeemed. We have that light that shines in us even in darkens (Psalm 27:1). We therefore fear nothing or no one. He carries us through the waters and rivers. He further sustains us through dark times and through fires (Isaiah 43:1-2).

There has to be forgiveness of sins in order to receive salvation. As mentioned in another section of this book, salvation comes through faith in Christ. After giving your life to Him, you are saved. There are many practical advantages to a Christian's lifestyle. Christianity sees another dimension of reality beyond the material world. Both realms are important, and both host forces that are at cross purposes with each other. How thankful we can be that we are promised victory. There is always mercy associated with giving your life to Christ (Sabbath afternoon, 2012)

The article published on the Sabbath afternoon of (2012) further suggest that the Christians would have no hope of victory over the forces of evil unless the stage was set for it. The stage was set by Christ through his death on the cross and His resurrection from the grave. His death and resurrection obtained victory for His people over all kinds of dark forces and principalities. In a very real sense, the unmasking and disarming of these evil forces have placed a limit on them. The fact that their powers have been brought under subjection through the death of Christ sets the stage for the victory of the Christians (Sabbath Afternoon, 2012). All this happens through faith. Jesus foretold in the writings of Matthew that if you have faith as little as a mustard seed, you can command a mountain to move to a yonder place. The critical aspect I picked up in Matthew is that our faith must be accompanied by prayer. When you pray, you must believe what you are asking has already been done. This then means you don't just wait upon the Lord in faith, but you also must pray in faith. Prayer done in faith produces results. Further that, in life there appear to be very stubborn spirits. Such spits need prayer, fasting and prayer (Matthew 17:20-21).

A certain man in the registers of Matthew brought his sick son to Jesus. His sickness caused him to fall on water or even on fire. This situation was really heartbreaking for the father. Instead of enjoying to see his son grow up in a normal way and achieving things like other boys did, he appeared to be a daily burden. The good thing about the father was that in the midst of that challenge, he kept on seeking help for his son. Scripture posit that the father had even taken his son to Jesus' disciples and they were not able to heal him even though they did lay hands on him Matthew 17:16). Jesus blamed his disciples for having no faith, but also he disclosed something interesting. He told them that some spirits can only be cast out through prayer and fasting (Mathew 17:21).

Some of the challenges we face may require for us to employ such a principle of prayer and fasting. Some opposition may appear not to change even after lots and lots of prayer. If such happens, we are given another principle to utilize. The weapon of prayer and fasting and this weapon is bound to bring fruitful results if used in faith. It is a weapon granted to us to fight against stubborn spirits and is free of charge. Towned and Getty (2012) pointed out that the power of the Cross is a meditation on the suffering of Christ. His suffering was through the hands of Pilate. Therefore a reminder is set as we partake of the Holy Communion to remember His death till His promised return. In their article Towned and Getty suggested that the suffering of Christ has been given a surface glance and not fully explored which then leads to the real theological meaning of the cross confused. They further add that the cross should be viewed in light of Christ becoming sin for his people and thus his people are redeemed and forgiven at the cross (Towned and Getty, 2012). There are many benefits of the cross recorded in scripture. The author of the book of Mark presents the elements of substitution nurture of Christ's work on the cross. We read of Barabbas in Mark who was an insurrectionist and a murderer. Yet despite his guilt and depravity, Barabbas was released from prison and in his place Jesus was immersed in a horrifying injustice and was sentenced to die (Thomas, 2022). In this pericope, Jesus had been betrayed and arrested. His disciples fled in fear, deserting Him and He was subjected to the judgment of Pilate. Jesus refused to defend himself. I bet he already knew that it was time for Him to pay the price for his people (Matthew 26:14-16, Mathew 26:47-56). It was destined for Him to go to the cross to fulfill the benefit of substitution. Jesus substituted himself for the guilty sinners who are his people (Sanchez, 2020). He therefore gave His life for us and while we were still sinners, Christ died for us

(Romans 5:8). As a result of His death on the cross, we can be victorious and can defeat any challenge. When He died on the cross he exchanged us and made us sanctified.

According to White (2021) this exchange was a way of sanctification to His people. Sanctification refers to God's unlimited and transcendent purity and beauty. He gleams over the universe like the sun in the sky and is full of glory. White further posit that the cross is a source of power that allows God's people to put the old ways in the past and restore true humanity. Such power leads to living a new life which exudes purity, holiness and is the best life that cannot be compared with anything (White, 2021). Christ's death is the evidence of our justification, the origin of our sanctification and the initiate of our glorification. Such sanctification is the hope of our eternal and complete victory (Gray, 2019). Through such knowledge therefore we can face any opposition with boldness knowing that we were redeemed with the precious blood of the Lord Jesus Christ (1 Peter 1:19).

In addition to Jesus paying the price for us Sanchez explored three other benefits of the cross. He suggested that at the Cross Jesus was taking our curse. It is mentioned in the gospel of Matthew that they plaited a crown of thorns, put it upon his head and a reed in his right hand. They mocked him saying hail King of the Jews (Mark 15:17, John 19:2-5). Sanchez revealed that in the earliest chapters of the Bible, the thorns were the results of the curse that had come into the world because sin (Genesis 3:17-18). Putting the thorns on his head therefore removed that curse from our lives. Scripture further reveal that the son refused to shine, such that there was total darkness on earth when Jesus died (Mark 15:33). Like thorns, the darkness during the day was a sign of God's curse due to sin (Deuteronomy 28:29). Jesus bore the thorns and darkness of our sins upon himself at the cross (Sanchez, 2020).

The other benefit of the cross is that Jesus was clothing us. The dividing of His garments among themselves, casting lots for them to decide what each should take and thus fulfilling the prophecy in Psalm (22:18). That dividing of his clothes signified Him clothing his people and covering his people with righteousness (Isaiah 61.10). Just because we are clothed with righteousness we are promised victory over opposition as recorded in annals of Isaiah. *'No weapon that is formed against thee shall prosper; and every tongue that shall rise against thee in judgment thou shalt condemn. This the heritage of the servants of the Lord, and their righteousness in of Me', saith the Lord (Isaiah 54:17).*

The last benefit of the cross Sanchez discussed was that of Jesus gashing heaven open for his people. The author of the book of Mark revealed that when Jesus died, the curtain of the temple was torn in two, from top to bottom (Mark 15:38). This curtain separated the holy of holies from the rest of the temple. In the holy of holies God's presence was mostly resolute. It was not everyone who was allowed to enter that place, but only the priest. But through His crucifixion that curtain was split into two signifying access to his presence for everyone and also to the heavenly sanctuary (Sanchez, 2020). When we have complete access to His presence we can therefore call upon him and pour out our hearts asking for every opposition to be impassive.

The Bible is crystal clear and expounds that God created us for his glory. *Thus says the Lord, "Bring my sons from afar and my daughters from the end of the earth, everyone who is called by my name, whom I created for my glory" (Isa. 43:6–7).* Life is wasted when we do not live for the glory of God. It is all for his glory that He sent His Son to die for us on the cross and ultimately giving us victory over sin and any other kind of opposition (Piper, 2018).

CHAPTER 4

THE POWER UNSEEN YET PREVAILENT

In the beginning was the Word, and Word was with God, and the Word was God. He was with God in the beginning. Through him all things were mad; without Him nothing was made that has been made. In Him was life, and that life was the light of mankind. The light shines in darkness and the darkness does not comprehend it (John 1:1-5).

Dark forces are prevalent in the world and that fact cannot be disputed. I started noticing dark forces while in High School. Although I had a bit understanding that there are evil forces based on my sickness, but I had never been directly visited by evil forces before. I only knew that my sickness was potentially a spiritual attack, but I had not dealt with evil forces directly until I got to high school. I was staying at the hostel and was a boarding student. As earlier mentioned in this book, I was now a firm believer in the Lord Jesus Christ but still growing in my quest for Him. In the night some spirits would come to the room I was staying in. There were four of us sharing a room as students. These dark forces would come and I would hear them coming while I was sleeping. The first time I heard these spirit approaching our room I was really terrified. I recall waking up just as the spirits were touching the door handle to open the door. I was soaking wet from sweat. It was like this was literally happening, and it was indeed factually happening. The spirits were really there. One may argue that it was only a dream, but I know for sure these were spirits. When I woke up that first day I couldn't sleep again in fear that these spirits will come again. I could hear them talking while approaching confirming that all they needed to do was to take me alive and their boss would know what to do next. Who would want to be taken away by unknown entities in the middle of the night? I stayed awake all night long. At first I never shared this encounter with anyone. I knew no one would believe me, or better still no one would take me seriously.

They came again the next day, and I realized that they would come after 12 midnight. On this particular day, I woke up my friend who was sleeping next to me. I knew that this was beginning to be a serious thing because they were now saying 'don't fail like yesterday'. When I narrated the story to my friend in the middle of the night, he suggested that we pray. After we had prayed, I realized that I found peace and the fear vanished. So I was able to sleep. From that time on, the spirits would come sometimes twice or thrice a week. But instead of waking my friend up, I started praying on my own every time I perceived them coming. They would only come when I was asleep and every time I would wake up and call upon the Lord. The Lord instructs us to call upon Him in the day of trouble, and promises to deliver us (Psalm 50:15). These forces seemed to be increasing in number because I would hear more and more voices as time went by and when I felt really threatened, I would wake up my friend to pray with me.

Not long after I discovered my attack at night, while we were in one of our services at the boarding school, one of the students manifested. He was screaming so loud that we had to hold him down and prayed for him. The stronger guys in the Lord at that time would be commanding the spirit to leave in the name of Jesus. After some time, the spirit would depart. The spirit would re-enter the student again such that during our next service, he would scream yet again. My own problems were not over yet. My attacks were still intensifying at night, but I was getting stronger and stronger in prayer such that they never won me over. Psalm (138. 7-8) states that though I walk in the midst of trouble, the Lord preserves my life, He stretches out His hand against the wrath of my enemies, and His right hand delivers me. The Lord fulfilled his promises for me. The steadfast love of the Lord, endures forever and He does not forsake the work of His hands (Psalm 138:8). Indeed the Lord protected me during those frustrating times.

The manifestation of the evil forces in that student culminated great fear amongst boarding students and the news reached the entire school. The spirit seemed to be attacking more students from then on and a word was spreading around that there were devil worshippers in the school. Through fear, a lot of students gave their lives to Christ, and the Student Fellowship grew in an alarming rate within a short space of time. Prayer was intensified and we even had a group of students who would wake up at 12 midnight to pray in the sports ground. I was one of those students and this gave me a chance to evade my own attacks. We were determined to nullify such spirits. I can safety say, God intervened, because such spirits seemed to have vanished and no one was manifesting anymore. The only challenge I observed was that the students who gave their lives to Christ during that period of attack, reverted back to their old ways when the threat was no more. The gist of the story is to show that evil forces do exist and they bring fear to many. They may not be seen by the naked eye, but their effects can be seen and felt.

Therefore we do not lose heart. Though outwardly we are wasting away, yet inwardly we are being renewed day by day. For our light and momentary trouble are achieving for us an internal glory that far outweighs them all. So we fix our eyes not on what is seen, but on what is unseen, since what is seen is temporary but what is unseen is eternal (2 Corinthians 4:16-18).

Focusing on the visible material things delays or hinders us from growing in the things of the Lord. The spirit of God is always available to us, but is not visible to the naked eye. The spirit renews us inwardly, it may appear as though we are wasting away as recorded in the verse above. Our bodies may appear stricken, but our spirit in the midst of pain is renewed and God gives us strength in weakness. Jesus told his disciples that as He was going away to be with the Father in heaven, he was leaving them with the Holy Spirit who will comfort them (John 14:16)

We are never really alone. So the enemy may think he got us all alone by causing all our friends to leave, but there in the midst of the loneliness comes the spirit of God comforting us day in and day out. Unseen yet present to guide and protect us. The death of Christ on the cross was worth it. As He left the earth after resurrection, He left his people with a powerful weapon. That weapon is the Holy Ghost. In actual fact, Jesus was living us with Himself. The knowledge that God is a unit consisting of the Father, the Son and the Holy Spirit, is sure affirmation that Jesus left His people with Himself. He further assured his people that he would never leave them nor forsake them (Hebrews 13:5). Just because we cannot physically see Him working in our lives does not mean he has left us or forgotten about us. When it appears like the situation we are facing is becoming worse and seems like he does not hear our prayers. We must always know that He is always there with us. This is because He promised never to leave us nor forsake. All we have to do is have faith in Him.

There are many things which are unseen in the world around us. Just because we don't see them does not mean they don't exist (Hatcher, 1994). The wind for instance is one phenomenon that exist but cannot be seen. The wind can be felt or better still people can tell there is wind by watching the effects it brings to nature. We can observe trees moving, grass stirring or dust sometimes can be seen. The dust itself is not the wind, but the dust is blown by the wind. Apart from that, wind can be felt by our bodies. We feel the breeze of air but cannot see it, let alone touch it.

It's the same thing with God. We can see His immaculate creation but we cannot see Him directly. For those who are spiritually inclined to Him, they feel His presence over their lives, but they don't see Him. The mystery of the presence of God is that is cannot be explained. The spiritual people can feel His presence and yet have difficulty in describing the feeling. His existence and supremacy can never be denied. *For since the creation of the world God's invisible qualities, His eternal power and divine nature have been clearly seen, being understood from what has been made, so that people are without excuse (Romans 1:20).*

This verse suggest that some people may have an excuse for not worshipping the Lord. One such excuse would be why worship someone unseen. But scripture has constantly given us assurance of his existence. Paul suggested that one of the easiest principles or mechanism of knowing God is real, is to look at His creation (Romans 1:18=1, Psalm 19:1-6). Arguing about the existence of God has no benefits at all. All those who have doubts about his existence should make reference to their own lives. It was surely not their parents who breathe the life inside of them. Again it was not their parents that allowed their eyes to see, their ears to hear, their mouth to speak, their legs to walk and their brain to think. The brain some people are now using to try and convince themselves and others that there is no God, was given to them by Him. The reality people don't realize is that life belongs to God and He may take it any time He pleases. The events of the Covid-19 pandemic were flawless proof that anyone can die at any given time. When your time to go has come, there is no amount of money that can stop you from dying. God has the power which is unseen to give life and also unseen power to take it.

The power of God unseen is able to fight for us battles we even don't know about. Singhji (2016) states that once we connect with God's power which is embedded deep inside of us through meditation, or just sitting still in silence and repeating the name of Jesues, we realize that we are not alone in this world after all. Singhji presents the power of mediation. Scripture also affirms that we should meditate on His word day and night (Joshua 1:8). His unseen hand always surrounds us. This gives us strength and encourages to face our challenges head-on.

Without a doubt human beings more especially those who believe in God know that there is more to life than what can be sensed through empirical processes. God Himself is a spirit and cannot be seen through a telescope or any other lenses. We believe in Him, His angels, but also acknowledge the existence of demons. Such demons are spiritual beings which could affect us in ways we can never imagine (Thorburn, 20212).

While analyzing the story of Daniel chapter 10, Thorburn uncovered that reality is in two folds. There is the visible world of kings and empires and wars and then on the other hand exist the invisible world of angels and heavenly beings. Tapping into the spiritual realms allows us to experience that unseen power of God and angels. When we experience that unseen power, we become content that indeed our savior lives and is always fighting our battles on our behalf.

4.2 The unanticipated journey

The Lord's appearance and calling in my life is a story I choose to exclude in this particular writing. It is a story to be shared another time and in another place. With that said, I have always been someone who had a zeal to study Theology. In actual fact, I studied the bible through correspondence in High School to a level of a Diploma. The longing to pursue more of bible studies never left me. It was not until the Lord appeared to me, that I started noticing some free theology lessons online. When I did thorough research, I was led to two particular institutions. Scrutinizing these institutions closer, I began to have a liking for Christian Leaders Institute which is an American Institution offering high quality education. I started taking some courses there. This was so exciting, I thought I was going to cruise through these courses and learn as much as possible. After a few courses, I realized how challenging Theology was. My perceptive on the whole Theology and Divinity concepts changed. My respect for the subjects increased and ultimately my respect for God also was enlarged. Every time I got a chance I would be studying, and learning new things in theology through Christian Leaders Institute. After about three years of my study and many courses later, another door was opened in my life. I was contacted by the President of the Life Changing and Bible Ministry University which is a Mentor Centre for Christian Leaders Institute through an email. That email was life altering. I joined Life Changing Bible and Ministry University to further my studies and the journey has been exquisite. The platform to learn for free and also the chance to preach on their platform is beyond words. This new journey which I never really anticipated has opened up endless possibilities and also helped me in overcoming some of the opposing factors in my life. Learning is one vital instrument to overcoming opposition. Some people are defeated by challenges because of lack of knowledge. Jesus also mentioned that His people are perishing because of lack of knowledge. Studying the word of God is key, but also acquainting yourself with other supportive literature to master Theology can greatly help you in overcoming opposition. Learning never ends and there is no age limit when it comes to learning the things of the Lord. This new journey that has been presented to me through Life Changing Bible and Ministry University has opened up this opportunity for me to write this book. A journey I did not anticipate. Now I know that the ways of the Lord cannot be understood. While researching about the content of this book, I have grown both in the things of God, in wisdom and also I'm now well prepared to fight any opposition until the Lord wins. He always wins no matter what.

CONCLUSION

This book touch on several critical elements of overcoming opposition in our lives. The author mostly explored biblical elements and gave personal examples by discussion personal encounters. Chapter one mostly dealt with discovering the opposing factors in our lives. You cannot defeat a problem you don't know. Acknowledging that there is a problem and identifying what the problem really is opens doors to dealing with it. It is easier to defeat an enemy you have identified. Once you know what you are dealing with, you can direct all your efforts in trying to ascertain the behavior of the problem, how it grows and it impact. Once you know all this it becomes easier to craft specific weapons to annihilate the problem. Not every fight needs a gun to win. If you are dealing with a nuisance rat in your house, you cannot not use a gun to shoot it. But you can identify the appropriate methods to kill a rat. We discovered also in this chapter that all opposition is submissive to God and thus we must intensify our efforts to rely on Him rather than our own efforts.

Just like the first chapter, chapter two also expanded further to explore biblical concepts of identifying opposition. Most archives of biblical giants were quoted and how they identified the problem. But also chapter two discussed not only identifying the problem, but also discovering the solution. A solution foreign to you cannot bring the anticipated results. Discovering God's grace is the instrument that can help you deal with opposition. Being far from Him inhibits the rewards associated with His grace. But drawing closer to Him opens doors and leads to miracles untold. Chapter three explored the benefits of Jesus dying on the cross. It revealed that crucifixion brought about the forgiveness of our sins. It was a place where Jesus exchanged Himself for our sins and thus we were justified and sanctified. Apart from justification and sanctification, chapter three highlighted that through His death we were made victorious. There is therefore no opposition that can stand against us because through Jesus, we are always triumphant. The amazing work of the cross further remove the curse of sin from our lives and Jesus also clothed us through His death. Finally chapter four expounded on the power of the unseen world. God is unseen yet always at work in our lives conquering all our challenges. However we must not be ignorant about the unseen evil world. Our role is to lean on the unseen God for us to stand against the unseen evil world.

POSTSCRIPT

Drawing conclusions about a person's life based on concepts emanating from a person's intelligence doesn't mean God has made the same conclusions. Real conclusions about a person's circumstances are determined by God as the Author and the Finisher of our faith. After all He is the one who gave us life and thus has full knowledge of when and how he will take it. He knows best and can be able to alter any human derived synopses. Trusting what people supposedly think about you, is reducing yourself into nothing at all. Have you placed your life in a jar of water when there is a whole ocean to swim in? There is interminable potential and victory in God, All you have to do is put your trust in Him as an unlimited supply. Allowing people to construe your destiny is ultimately reducing the promises given to us by God. There is a God who is all knowing and all perfect who can give you a better meaning in life. Opposition should not be viewed as what is destined for your life, but should be viewed in the parameters of a channel that leads to greater executions.

This book has made reference to his word which is a perfect guide in dealing with any kind of challenge. The promises of God crafted in His word are endless, showing us that He is also endless. He goes from glory to glory. Why then reduce your life to listening to deceits when there are profound truths found in His word? Listening to someone who bases his theories on what he has studied on paper is selling yourself short. Why do you trust conclusions made by a mortal entity when there exist that which is immortal and founded everything. Real victory is found in the perfect hand of Jehovah who was there even before our forefathers ever existed. That's the real power of success. True success is breath when you start believing God and His truth. Believing anything else is only a roadway to destruction. Not everyone you trust can recommend reality and true reality is the belief in the supernatural. After all human beings are only spirits planted in the body. This is also known to the ones who believe in ancestors. The ancestors are believed to be speaking to people even while in their graves. It was only the body that was buried but the spirit lives on. Just as the good book specifies that there is coming a time for eschatology. The judged will not be the bodies, but the spirits embedded in the bodies. Indeed the Lord is coming again and shall not delay (Hebrews 10:37). The fascinations of this world will only remain here on earth and the spirit shall live on. This is a very profound motif that every man ought to ponder on staid bases. The eschatology motif is one that many evade. They seemed to be focusing on vanity things which are only meant for this world. The eyes of many have been blinded such that their only focus is on material things which have no eternal gain (John 12:40). True victory is earning your place with God. To live is Christ and to die is gain (Philippians 1:21).

Therefore we should count it all joy when we are persecuted knowing that our true victory is in him. While awaiting his return, practice his word and his promises of which some of them are crafted in this book. The aim of this book is to bring direction or recommendations on attaining victory in opposition. The author did not craft his own thinking but tried to construe conclusions based on scripture which brings lasting solutions. Psychological concepts are great and has assisted a lot of people to deal with their skeletons. It is a subject that brings solutions, but such solutions are only temporal.

There is however a lasting solution to all problems and it is rooted all over scripture. If you can only open your eyes you will see.

REFERENCES

Gray, A. (2019). Six Benefits believers receive from Christ's death. Reformation Scotland, pp. 2. Available from: www.reformationscotland.org. [Accessed on March 2022].

Chapel, F. (2022). I have been crucified with Christ. It is Christ who lives in me –Galatians 2:20). Available from: www.agfaithchapel.org. [Accessed on October, 2022], pp. 1.

Gordon, I. (2022). Isaiah Chapter 43: God will make a Way. Isaiah bible series. Book. Jesus plus Nothing, pp1. Available from: www.jesusplusnothing.com.

Hatcher, W. 1994). A Scientific Proof of the Existence of God. Journal of Bahai Studies vol. 5, number 4, pp.5. First published in Russia in 1992.

Kadari, T. (1999). The Shalvi/ Hyman Enclopedia of Jewish Women. Peninnah: Midraash and Aggadah. Jewish Women's Archive, pp.2. Available from: www.jwa.org.

Kamelia (2022). Is God Real? The Unseen Ancient Power. Common Questions and Discussions. Available from: www.bahaiblog.net. [Accessed on 3 August 2022].

Squires, J, T. (2022). An Informed Faith. Jesus, Barabbas, son of the father: freedom fighter, or fable? (Holy Week). Australia. Available from: www.johnsquires.com.

Piper, J. (2018). Don't Waste Your Life. Book. Crossway. Wheaton. Illinois. United States, pp. 28. First printed in 2003. Reprinted in 2018.

Richard, M, G. (2022). The Doctrine of Creation. An Essay. Concise Theology Series. Licensed under CC BY-SA 4.0, pp. 1.

Ruse, M. (2009). Charles Darwin on Human evolution, Journal of Economic Behaviour and Organisation. Volume 71, issue 1 July 2009, pp. 12.

Sanchez, A. (2020). 4 Benefits Jesus Gives you at the cross. Core Christianity. Sandiego, United States of America. 17 March, 2020. Available from: www.corechristianity.com.

Singhji, S, R. (2016). Mystic Mantra: God's unseen arm is always around us. Deccan Chronicle. Article. Available from: www.deccanchronicle.com.

Thorburn, T. (2021). The Unseen World. The Gospel Coaliation. Article. Available from: www.au.thegospelcoaliation.org.

Towned, S and Getty, K. (2012). The Power of the Cross. Discipleship ministries. The United Methodist Church. United States of America. Available from: www.umcdiscipleship.org.

White, W. (2021). The Amazing Benefits of the Cross: Sanctification (Romans 6:1-14). Evergreen Church. Available from: www.evergreetn.com.

I want morebooks!

Buy your books fast and straightforward online - at one of world's fastest growing online book stores! Environmentally sound due to Print-on-Demand technologies.

Buy your books online at
www.morebooks.shop

Kaufen Sie Ihre Bücher schnell und unkompliziert online – auf einer der am schnellsten wachsenden Buchhandelsplattformen weltweit! Dank Print-On-Demand umwelt- und ressourcenschonend produziert.

Bücher schneller online kaufen
www.morebooks.shop

Printed by Books on Demand GmbH, Norderstedt / Germany